YO-AEV-949

A Busy Mom's Guide

100 Easy Ways to Get Your Kids Reading

WITHDRAWN

Kathleen Duey

Illustrated by Jacob Dubi

ROCKFORD PUBLIC LIBRARY

©2006 BiG GUY BOOKS, Inc.
ALL RIGHTS RESERVED

No part of this publication may be reproduced, modified, or transmitted
in any form, electronic or mechanical, including photocopying
or digital scanning, without specific permission from the publisher.

Typeset in Futura and Wide Latin.

ISBN: 1-929945-65-5

Library of Congress Control Number: 2005935056

Published by BiG GUY BOOKS, Inc.
6359 Paseo Del Lago • Ste B
Carlsbad, CA 92011 USA

Printed in USA

ACKNOWLEDGMENT

- - - - - - - - - -

I know most mothers (and fathers) have to squeeze parenting into the hours before and after their *other* full-time jobs. This book is dedicated to you.

Thanks for making time to get your kids reading!

A child's ability to learn, get good grades, and build self-esteem can depend on good reading skills. Job choices, career advancement, and income level are all effected by reading ability.

Reading is incredibly important. It's that simple.

Getting your child to read can be simple, too...

CHALLENGED READERS

- - - - - - - - - -

If your child is having trouble reading, get help. Schools—and most communities—have resources to help any child read better. Ask teachers and librarians what is available. Remind your child that no one is good at everything. Encourage reading. Praise and support your child's efforts.

> ## To Get Started
>
> The International Reading Association (IRA) has resources at:
>
> http://www.reading.org/resources/tools/index.html
>
> Download IRA pamphlets at:
>
> http://www.reading.org/resources/tools/parent.html
>
> Other helpful websites include:
>
> http://www.rif.org
>
> http://www.literacyconnections.com

RELUCTANT READERS

- - - - - - - - -

Children watch TV for information and entertainment. Choices are nearly endless—comedy, music, heart-tugging drama, experts giving advice on almost anything. Films, videos, and video games compete for their attention, too. So why focus on reading?

One important fact stands out: The vast majority of smart, entertaining, and informative people lived before the age of video. Their knowledge isn't available on TV. It is housed in libraries. If your child can read but doesn't, he is no better off than someone who can't read at all.

Evidence is mounting that reading exercises parts of the brain that watching video images doesn't. Imagination is hard to quantify, but when I ask an auditorium full of school kids to help me build a storyline, it sometimes takes a long time to get ideas that aren't from a TV show or video game.

You can help reluctant readers find their own reasons to read. There are resources in almost every community.

Helpful Websites

International Reading Association resources:
http://www.reading.org/resources/tools/parent.html
For boys: Author Jon Scieszka Guys Read project:
http://www.guysread.com
Mike Sullivan's Connecting Boys with Books:
http://www.talestoldtall.com/BoyParents.htm

LET THE FUN BEGIN!

Books are ice cream, not medicine. Reading is a joy. Literacy is the ticket to everything the human race has ever learned about life, the world, and our own hearts. This book will help you offer reading to your kids in the same way you would offer them something delicious, something fun, something you know they will like.

USING THIS BOOK

The activities and reading tips in this book are intended to fit into your daily life. Every section contains reader-friendly ideas for different ages and skill levels. In each section, look for the age group that fits your child—but be flexible. You might have a "tween-ager" who still loves riddle books, or a five-year-old who will choose detailed dinosaur facts instead of a story any day. Whatever increases reading—and fun—is the right choice. Encourage young readers to become self-propelled. Help them find their own reasons to read. The Bookspeak chapter of this book lists awards, sources, book terms, kids' magazines, and more. Check it out when you have time!

Ready to get your kids reading? Here we go.

TABLE OF CONTENTS

Baby Steps to Reading

When should you start reading to your baby? As soon as you can! Babies love the sound of your voice; the warmth of your lap; eye contact; and warm, loving attention. Reading with your baby can help develop listening skills and begin a lifelong feeling of comfort and warmth associated with reading and books.

1. Get cozy. For the newest newborns, use bath time, naptime, and quiet time to read and play. Turn off radios and TVs, cuddle up, then sing, talk, tell stories, and repeat rhymes. The sound of your voice and the rhythm of the words will help your baby begin to learn about language, with or without a book at first. For fun rhymes and rhythms, use Wee Willie Winkie or This Little Piggy or other rhymes you remember from your childhood. Then go exploring. Ask older family members. Look for nursery rhyme books at any bookstore or your library.

> Google it: "*nursery rhymes*"
> (Include the quotes to narrow and focus your search.)

2. Older newborns can be propped in the crook of your arm or settled on your chest, looking toward the open book. Babies will happily stare at colorful pictures while you read aloud—or simply retell a story in your own words. Listen to and react to your child's sound-making with smiles and attention.

1. Holding Her Own. **Babies who can sit up without support can hold a book. If they have been read to and have seen people reading, they already know how it is done. Board books are a perfect beginner's book. With thick, reinforced pages, they can be held, dropped, pounded, worn, thrown, and chewed—a perfect introduction to the many joys of reading!**

2. Pointers. **If you are not already doing it, point at familiar objects in book art and name them. Your baby will begin to try to repeat the names as time goes on. Reading together is a natural beginning for language learning. If you make any motions or sounds at certain points in the story, encourage your child to imitate them. Simple concepts of size and motion can be learned from storybooks.**

> Ex. "Then the sun came up in the big, *wide* sky..."
> **(Make a slow, sweeping motion with one hand.)**

3. Longer Reading Sessions. **Once a baby is old enough to sit unassisted in your lap, you can read longer books or several books. Ham it up! Make faces, do voices, enjoy the funny stories and the dreamy, softer tales. Show your baby how much you like reading and how much fun it can be.**

4. Favorites and Rejects. **Even babies will let you know what their favorites are— and which books they don't like. Respect their feelings. One of the many joys of reading is the joy of choice.**

1. **Encore!** Babies and very young children love to hear the same books over and over. Grin and begin again! Learning is a process of repetition. Once the book is familiar, you can sometimes make a game out of posing questions to your toddler.

> Did the moon turn green? Was the bunny hopping? **etc.**

2. **Bedtime Stories.** For most children, favorites are books that can be read at bedtime. If your child's favorite isn't a calming read, try reading it first, followed by one or two quieter books.

3. **Shapes and Colors.** Begin to point out colors, shapes, and relative size in the art. Ask questions: "Is that a BIG apple?" "Which jacket is red?" Keep it fun.

4. **Baby's Book Nook.** Bookshelves for an older child might seem obvious, but a special place to keep your baby's books is a good idea, too. Babies can learn (slowly!) that books are special, important, and worthy of careful handling. They can also "read" independently if they can reach their board books themselves.

5. **Ready to Read.** You can use reading time to begin to learn the alphabet. There are many, many (many!) great alphabet books. Ask a librarian or a bookseller to recommend a few that might intrigue your baby.

Choosing Books for Your Baby

For younger babies, look for:

1. Simple words and concepts
2. Bright, distinct art
3. Pictures your baby will recognize. Look for art that features babies, pets, clothing, household items, cars, trucks, moon, sun, trees, etc.
4. Sturdy paper and bindings. Board books can be "read" alone.

Ask any bookseller, educator, or librarian for recommendations.

As your baby grows:

1. Attention span lengthens so language can be more complex, art more detailed.
2. You can talk more about the pictures in the books, so look for art with natural interaction possibilities. Ex. "There's a dog. He's brown like Tim's dog, isn't he? Yes! He's a brown dog."
3. As you learn what your child likes, make sure you both accommodate the baby's taste and, gently, broaden it. Don't begin a battle of wills if your child insists on the same book or two over and over for a time, though. The idea is to keep reading fun for both of you.
4. Take your baby to the bookstore. Let her have a say in what you buy for her.
5. Be a good role model and bring your own book! You can sometimes read side by side with your baby for a little while.
6. Have fun! Reading with your baby will be a memory that you treasure forever.

Good Morning, Readers!

Here's how you can start every day with reading.

6-up Rain or Shine?

Have your child read a weather report aloud in the morning. Internet weather sites provide a quick printout the night before if you don't take a morning paper. Or have her read a weather forecast aloud in the evening so everyone knows what to wear the next day!

6-8 Cereal Reading: Back of the Box

Nearly every cereal box has writing on the back. Some are more interesting than others, but most provide text your child can read aloud at the breakfast table.

All ages Serial Reading

Every reader in the house can take a turn reading a few pages or a few paragraphs of a story for the whole family each morning. If mornings are too hectic, this makes a good evening activity, too.

All ages A Poem a Day

Start every day with a poem! Your child can read it aloud at the breakfast table. Or you can read aloud, asking your emerging reader to stand close and read a few words out of the poem as you go. Ask a teacher or a librarian to recommend a poetry anthology written at an appropriate age level.

6-up   Riddle Me This

Books of riddles make wonderful read-aloud fare for your child at the breakfast table (or in the car!). Riddles encourage creative thinking and reading fluency. Most bookstores and libraries shelve them in the humor section.

6-9   You're Joking?

Joke books delight some young readers. If yours likes to laugh, get read-aloud recommendations from a school or public librarian.

7-up   The Daily Facts

Daily calendars come with interesting facts about sports, weather, science, history, animals, and a wide range of other topics.

Follow your children's interests!

7-up Nutrition Wake Up Call

Reading labels on food packaging is a good habit. To get started, have your older readers announce the contents of their favorite cereal. Just reading the list of sweeteners and preservatives can often begin a family conversation about better eating habits. In case the two most common preservatives aren't spelled out, tell your child that BHT stands for butylated hydroxytoluene and BHA stands for butylated hydroxyanisole!

7-up Recipe Reads

Most of us don't cook elaborate breakfasts, but if you have a weekend pancake tradition—or during evening cooking—have your readers assist by reading recipes or other cooking directions aloud.

Anyone who reads can learn to cook well!

Playing lighthearted phonics games can sharpen skills and include your youngest readers in the fun. Try these, then make up your own:

First Letter: A call-and-response game

Point at any familiar object in the room and pronounce the name clearly.

Ex. "Toaster." Your child responds with the answer.

"It starts with 'T.'" Point to another object and repeat.

The pattern shouldn't be rigid. Interrupt the game for praise, acknowledgment, and fun. Switch roles, have your child find several things that begin with the same letter, re-invent the rules, keep it fun.

Vowel Voices (another call-and-response game)

You vocalize a long "A" sound "AAAA."

Your child repeats the sound and calls out a long "A" word like ape, grape, or sale.

Need help? Teachers can recommend phonics workbooks or give you practice sheets to give you game ideas. Many children's bookstores carry teacher's supplies—or can tell you where to find them.

Google it: "phonics games"
(Include the quotes to narrow and focus your search.)

All ages Reader Roll Call

Morning can become a time to ask what the family is reading and if everyone is enjoying it. Longer discussions can be left for evenings or weekends. For your youngest readers, this simple activity demonstrates that older children and adults are making reading part of their lives. School-assigned reading counts, as do novels or how-to books, poetry, political essays, bestsellers, or anything else you might be reading. Show (don't just tell) your kids that there are endless reasons to read.

8-up News They Can Use

Newspaper articles make great breakfast reading. Many adults read—or at least skim—a newspaper every morning. Learning about world events and national concerns should be part of every reader's—every citizen's—reading experience. Let your older readers take turns picking news articles to read aloud to the whole family.

If there isn't time on weekday mornings, consider weekends or evenings.

6-up Newspaper Comics

Most newspapers have a comics page. For younger readers, sharing a few comics can be a great way to start the day, too. If you have a reader who loves cartoons, consider buying books by favorite cartoonists.

8-up What's Up Locally

In smaller cities and towns, the local newspaper often includes news about people you know. In big cities, free papers dealing with local happenings are often distributed in neighborhoods. School newsletters might interest everyone as well. Your morning read-aloud time can be a community update.

All ages Kids' News!

KIDS' NEWS SOURCES

Weekly Reader
Weekly Reader produces news magazines especially for kids. Check them out.

For elementary students:
http://www.weeklyreader.com/ store/elem.asp

For middle and high schoolers:
http://www.weeklyreader.com/ store/sec.asp

Scholastic News for Kids
World news written for kids. Includes links and great articles.
http://teacher.scholastic.com/ scholasticnews/

New York Times for Kids
Amazing resource of great writing and information kids can understand.
http://www.nytimes.com/ learning/students/

CNN.com Student News
CNN provides international news for students. Includes links and more.
http://fyi.cnn.com/fyi/

Yahooligans News for Kids
Readers will find links to news aimed at school kids.
http://www.yahooligans.com/ content/news/

Science News for Kids
Covers every area of science news. Wonderful articles—and an archive.
http://www.sciencenewsforkids.org

Read and Roll: Making Car Time Count

The average American logs hundreds of hours of drive time every year. For busy mothers, much of that time is spent with children along for the ride. Whether it's your daily commute or the biannual trip to see Great-Aunt Betty three hours away, some of your car time can be used to make sure you are raising readers. Here are some ideas to get you rolling.

Find a good book bag for the car. Or two. Or one for each child. Ask each child to put in something they would like to read. Add riddle, joke, and fun fact books. If you have magazine readers, add recent issues of their favorites. Be sure the bag(s) contain something for every one of your passengers, including car-pool kids. Remind them that the books are available. Once a month, update the selections. Use update day as a chance to ask what the readers want to include. Don't forget to bring a book for yourself in case you end up waiting along the way.

CAR-TIME SKILL BUILDERS
- - - - - - - - - -

If you have beginning readers in your family, check with their teachers to see what reading skills are currently being taught in class. Ask what skills your child needs to practice. Shape these games accordingly—or make up your own!

4-6 Alphabet Soup

Young children can watch license plates and signs, finding each letter of the alphabet in sequence. If you have more than one beginning reader, have them take turns to keep the shouting down.

5-6 The First Letter Game

Call out a simple word and ask what letter it begins with. Again, with more than one reader, have them take turns responding. If you have an older reader on board, he can make up the words or use this list:

Ape	Boy	Oh	Pat
Cat	Dog	Quiet	Rat
Eat	Fan	Sun	Tip
Go	Hop	Use	Vine
Inch	Jump	Wipe	X-ray
Kick	Long	Yawn	
Mother	Nail	Zebra	

5-7 Phonics on Wheels

Using road and business signs that you pass, ask younger readers to look for words with repeated consonants, a long "u" sound, a short "e" sound, a blended consonant sound (sh sp, bl, etc.). A phonics workbook can provide ideas—any teacher can recommend a good one. If contests are handled well by your family, offer a small prize and keep score.

5-7 Seek and Speak

For older readers, try these variations:

Look for words with two syllables, or three!

Look for words with double consonants.

Find silent vowel words. Find nouns, adjectives, verbs, etc.

Find long "a," short "a," long "e," short "e," etc.

Give your children a "key word." Ask them to find words on signs that rhyme with the key word, have the same vowel sound, have the same first letter as the key word, etc.

Your children (or the car-pool kids) can take turns reading a book aloud. Choose a book that will interest everyone. You can award the privilege of picking the books or simply take turns picking. Or you can involve everyone in selection. Have them take turns reading a few pages of several candidate books. Encourage both readers and listeners to talk about what has been read aloud. This isn't a class—no one will be graded. ALL opinions—including complete disinterest in a book—are valid. Once they settle on a book, they can take turns reading aloud while you roll. (Reminder: Some people cannot read in cars without feeling sick. No one should feel forced!)

Here are some sample discussion points when choosing a book:

1. Did the first few pages hold your attention?

2. What do you know about the protagonist? Is he or she likeable? Silly? Sad? Scared? Funny? Angry? Rich? Poor? Make a list.

3. Did the book seem interesting?

4. Do you want to read the rest of the book to find out what happens?

If reading a book seems daunting or impractical, ask a teacher, librarians, or a bookstore employee to help you find an anthology of short stories appropriate for your drive-time readers.

Readers' theater is an adaptation of a book meant to be read aloud by several readers. Each child has a part, sometimes two. Many scripts are available in libraries and are leveled so you can match your readers' skills. Many teachers have favorites that are classroom-tried and true. Scripts for every level of reader are readily available on the Internet, many posted by teachers.

Aaron Shepard, a well-known children's author and a longtime readers' theater advocate, has published books of scripts you can purchase, but also offers many free, printable scripts on his website along with information about readers' theater.

Many are designed for classrooms, so there are many parts—sometimes as many as 20. Look for scripts with 4 to 8 parts and double up, if needed. Try it, you'll like it! And so will your readers.

Google it: "*readers' theater.*"
(Include the quotes to narrow and focus your search.)

You will find hundreds of websites with great information and scripts!

Aaron Shepard's website: *http://www.aaronshep.com/*

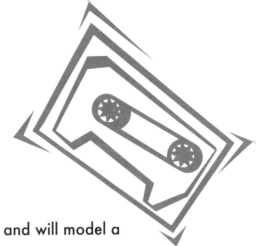

All ages STOP, LOOK, LISTEN: Books on Tape

Audio books can make longer trips more entertaining and will model a

smooth and fluent out-loud reading style. Listening to a riveting read-aloud can interest

your readers in books by the same author. Books on tape allow younger readers to

listen to more complex stories than they can read. Libraries often have books on

tape.

Google it: "*books on tape*" for more audio book rentals and sales
(Include the quotes to narrow and focus your search.)

All ages GET CREATIVE: Street Sign Stories

Have your passengers construct stories with words found on the signs you pass. They can add words to make the sign words connect sensibly or—just for fun—nonsensically.

Example (the "found" words are in italics):

A *restaurant* owner made a...(it becomes the next child's turn to add a sign word)... huge *doughnut*. It was bigger than a...(next child's turn)...*parking garage* and it filled the whole restaurant so that no one could come in. The owner decided to...(etc.)

Remember, the idea is to have fun and let ideas and creativity run wild. Silly IS good!

7-up GET LOCAL! Community Search

Use the Internet and your local newspaper to find out more about your town. Hotels and motels often have racks of pamphlets about interesting local attractions. Your kids can read about botanical gardens, museums, zoos, landmarks, an architectural wonder, or a family-run bakery. Check for printable websites. Have your child (or children, taking turns) read aloud as you drive—or at home.

If your kids are interested in any aspect of your town's history, make a library trip. Libraries often have real or microfilmed copies of newspapers from your town's past. Oral history projects will contain memories of local people. Most towns have historical societies, chambers of commerce, hobbyist clubs, and other organizations that might interest your kids. Family research projects encourage self-propelled reading and self-guided learning.

- - - - - - - - - -

There are reading opportunities in every errand. Here are a few ideas to get you started.

6-8 Fast Food, Fast Read

If you stop for food, ask your young readers to read the menu, even if they already know what they want.

6-8 Appoint a List Master

Make it your young readers' job to help you manage an errands list. Writing down, ordering, and crossing off errand items can help early readers understand how writing and reading help adults manage their lives.

6-8 Showtime/Gametime

At the video/videogame store online or in town, ask your kids to read the summaries of appropriate movies and games before they choose a video. Ask questions to improve their comprehension skills.

FRENCH FRIES

WORD GAMES

- - - - - - - - - -

Even though they don't directly involve reading, word games build language skills—and memory. Here are two of the classics.

6-up ## My Aunt is Moving...

First Child:
"My aunt is moving to New York
and she is taking apples with her."
(or any other object that begins with the letter A)

Second Child:
"My aunt is moving to New York and she is
taking apples and beans."

Third Child:
(or back to the first if you only have two players)
"My aunt is going to New York and she is taking apples,
beans, and cats."

And so on through the alphabet. There are many variations of this game. Let your children modify it to suit themselves!

5-up **I am Thinking Of...**

One person begins the game by saying, "I am thinking of an animal." (Or a fruit or a city or a dessert or a book or whatever can be reasonably guessed by the other players.)

Then the others take turns asking yes or no questions. A turn ends when the answer is "no." Then the questioner can guess or pass.

Example

Game initiator	Second player's questions
"I am thinking of an animal."	"Does it live in Africa?"
	"Yes."
First player's questions	"Does it have a long tail?"
	"No."
"Does it have fur?"	"I have a guess. Is it a hyena?"
"Yes."	"No."
"Does it eat meat?"	
"Yes."	
"Is it a wolf?"	
"No."	
"I pass."	

Games like this entertained generations of children before radio, TV, and computers were invented. Have your kids ask their grandparents or older neighbors about word games they played as children. Check your library for a book about the topic. Reasoning and language skills are important for every child, and words games are a fun and easy way to increase both!

TONGUE TWISTERS

Tongue twisters are a great way to polish speaking and pronunciation skills. This is my personal favorite, sung to the tune of a familiar old hymn.

All ages "Glory, Glory, How Peculiar"

Verse 1
One sly snake slid up the slide while the other sly snake slid down.
One sly snake slid up the slide while the other sly snake slid down.
One sly snake slid up the slide while the other sly snake slid down.
One sly snake slid up the slide while the other sly snake slid down.

Chorus
Glory, glory, how peculiar. Glory, glory, how peculiar. Glory, glory, how peculiar.
One sly snake slid up the slide while the other sly snake slid down. (Sing fast to fit!)

Verse 2
One eager eagle eased under the eaves while the other eager eagle eased east.
One eager eagle eased under the eaves while the other eager eagle eased east.
One eager eagle eased under the eaves while the other eager eagle eased east.
One eager eagle eased under the eaves while the other eager eagle eased east.

Chorus
Glory, glory, how peculiar. Glory, glory, how peculiar. Glory, glory, how peculiar.
One eager eagle eased under the eaves while the other eager eagle eased east.

Verse 3
One black bug bled blue-black blood while the other black bug bled blue.
One black bug bled blue-black blood while the other black bug bled blue.
One black bug bled blue-black blood while the other black bug bled blue.
One black bug bled blue-black blood while the other black bug bled blue.

Chorus
Glory, glory, how peculiar. Glory, glory, how peculiar. Glory, glory, how peculiar.
One black bug bled blue-black blood while the other black bug bled blue.

MORE TONGUE TWISTERS

Say These Five Times—FAST!

Toy boat

Unique New York

Red leather, yellow leather

Rubber baby buggy bumpers

How much wood would a woodchuck chuck
if a woodchuck could chuck wood?

The sheik bought six sick sheep.

Feminine, cinnamon, aluminum

Do anemones in the sea see enemy anemones?

Red lorry, yellow lorry

There are thousands of traditional tongue twisters. If your children enjoy them, find library books they can use as resources, and encourage them to make up their own!

Google it: "*tongue twisters*" for over a million hits!
(Include the quotes to narrow and focus your search.)

Online: http://www.uebersetzung.at/twister/ has tongue twisters in 107 languages!

- - - - - - - - - -

Peter Piper picked a peck of pickled peppers.
If Peter Piper picked a peck of pickled peppers,
where's the peck of pickled peppers Peter Piper picked?

- - - - - - - - - -

Betty Botter had some butter,
"But," she said, "this butter's bitter.
If I bake this bitter butter,
it would make my batter bitter.
But a bit of better butter—
that would make my batter better."

So she bought a bit of butter,
better than her bitter butter,
and she baked it in her batter,
and the batter was not bitter.
So 'twas better Betty Botter
bought a bit of better butter.

If your kids enjoy word play, collect favorites from relatives and friends, then hit the library for books of fun.

Google it: "*jump rope rhymes*" for hundreds of rhythmic rhymes to master.
(Include the quotes to narrow and focus your search.)

School Stuff

Success in most school subjects depends on reading skills. There are parent-child reading opportunities in every school activity and assignment. Here are a few to get you started.

7-up The Daily Update

Have your child read the day's homework assignments out loud on the way home, or as soon as possible after school. This helps you stay in touch with your child's workload and reminds the student of priority assignments. Many children have more trouble organizing homework than they have doing it. Explore list-making, a bedroom chalkboard, and other organizational tools. Find study skills books in your library.

6-up Handouts

School handouts can be read aloud in the car or at home. For younger readers, alternating between you (reading a paragraph) and them (reading a sentence) makes the information easier to absorb. As with all shared reading, be aware of your child's comfort level. Challenges are good, but too much criticism damages confidence—and of course, every child is different. Keep it fun.

When you have time, at least once in every school year, read a story or a book that your child has been assigned. Talk about it before, during, and after. The discussions don't need to be formal or long, or even especially deep. The fact that you have read a book your child has read means that you have a common experience, a secret bond. This is one of the joys of reading. Share it with your child.

7-up Feel The Drafts

The first draft of any of your child's written assignments can make good parent-child reading. Read the work aloud to your child—or the reverse. You can offer suggestions if that works well for both of you. High praise for excellence, for improvement, for seriousness of purpose, for any reason—works wonders. Your local library is well-stocked with books about writing skills. Revision is a key writing skill. Published books have usually gone through several revisions. Revision is one professional stunt you can try at home.

All ages Classroom Library

Many teachers use their own money to build classroom libraries. When I was a child, my favorite teacher, Mrs. Fredericksen, had a wonderful collection of books—and it influenced me forever. If your child's teacher has an in-room library, support it. When you weed your home collection, ask the teacher if any of the titles would be welcomed.

End of year gifts for a teacher can include books for the in-room library. I met a father who had organized a "one book per child" year-end gift. Each family brought a copy of their student's favorite book—some were good used copies—signed as a gift from the child to the teacher. She cried. Helping build school, public, and classroom libraries is an investment in your children, your community, your country, your world.

I speak nationwide at schools and I get to meet many school librarians. They are wonderful, dedicated people who work hard to make sure our children become literate. Sadly, many schools can no longer afford a full-time librarian. Some depend entirely on parent and grandparent volunteers who are wonderful people who might— or might not—have a background in children's literature. If there is a librarian in your child's school—or a volunteer with a background in teaching and children's books—ask for book recommendations.

Have your pen and paper ready!

A vibrant library is the heart of any school.

If you can, find ways to support yours.

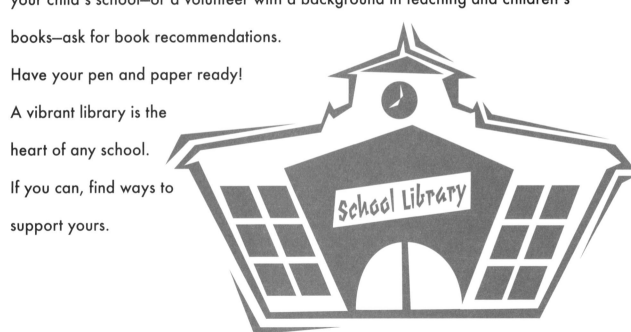

Homework and reading are easier when a child has a comfortable study place. Make sure your child has:

1. A writing surface big enough to hold an open book and a piece of paper with a little room to spare. A desk is great. A table will do.

2. Good light. If overhead lighting isn't enough, get a desk lamp.

3. A comfortable chair that is the right height.

4. Nonglare surfaces to minimize eyestrain.

5. A footrest for any student who can't comfortably touch the floor.

All ages Supplies

Pens, paper, pencils, erasers, crayons, and craft supplies should be as organized as possible. Rulers, compasses, and erasers—all standard homework tools—should be easy to find. If drawer space is limited, compartmentalized plastic storage bins are inexpensive and indestructible. Books on student organization and study skills are available in any public library, of course.

6-up Calendars

A school-year wall calendar is a great place to write due dates and other reminders. Help younger students with updates. A glance at the calendar can remind your student of upcoming due dates—and save late-night marathons.

All ages "To-Do" Lists

A pad of lined paper makes it easy for students to write lists of what they need to do—and to cross out the entries as projects are finished. Lists are a fundamental part of many adults' effort at time management. See if lists help your child.

5

While You Wait...

Every busy mom's life includes periods of waiting. Fast-food lines, soccer matches, traffic, rained-out activities, doctor's/dentist's offices...and more traffic. Here are some ideas for turning wait time into reading time.

All ages Open that Book Bag!

Unexpected waiting time is a perfect opportunity for your child to read his "car book" (novels, nonfiction, whatever is in the book bag). Here are a few more ideas for wait-time reading.

7-up Short and Sweet

Short stories are wonderful for unexpected reading opportunities. Young adult and teen readers have many to choose from—anthologies have enjoyed a rebirth over the past five years. If you are lucky enough to have an independent bookstore near you, ask what's new and what's good.

All ages Poetry

Poetry is a friend in the rain, the sound of distant thunder, the smell of your own kitchen, and so much more.

Dr. Seuss and Shel Silverstein are popular after all these years because their words rollick and bounce and make kids (and adults) laugh. There are many excellent poets who write for children. Some are astoundingly original, others comforting and familiar. Poems are usually short and often spark discussions. They can be laid aside the moment the wait is over and revisited later. Ask a librarian, teacher, or an independent bookseller for recommendations. You can also find many resources online.

Google it: *"poetry for children"*
(Include the quotes to narrow and focus your search.)

6-9 Riddles

Riddles make perfect waiting companions. The books are usually affordable paperbacks, slim and lightweight. Take turns reading aloud. Or, if you have a real "riddle master" in your family, let that person run the show.

All ages Jokes

Reading jokes aloud can change the mood from bored to bright. Many joke books are paperback and affordable. Collections of cartoons are great to share when you have a few minutes to wait.

All ages Fact Books

Can you name the rarest pine tree
on earth? Do kangaroos really box?
What hockey player scored the most
unassisted goals in 1994? Amazing facts
are perfect for a mixed-age group.
Take turns reading and listening to facts
about animals, sports, dinosaurs,
car racing—whatever interests your children.

All ages Record Books

Ripley's Believe It or Not and other fun and weird record books can work perfectly
when you only have a few minutes.

SKILL BUILDERS

(Learn while you wait!)

- - - - - - - - -

All ages Word Games

Word games are designed to entertain and pass time. The bonus is that they sharpen reading skills, too. Books of crosswords, word searches, and jumbled-letter puzzles for all skill levels are available in most bookstores. Don't forget to keep a few pencils in the car.

5-10 Guessing games and tongue twisters are great for unexpected waiting time, too.

Check CHAPTER THREE: READ AND ROLL for specific ideas!

5-7 Flash Cards

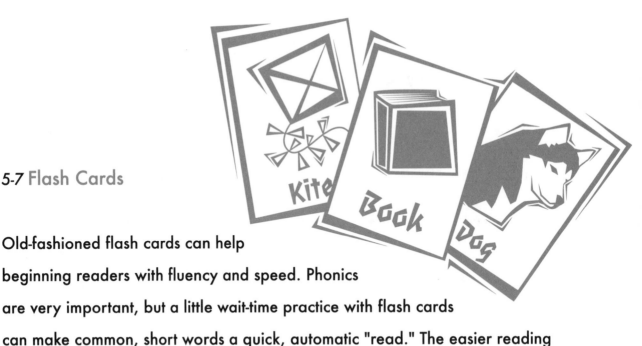

Old-fashioned flash cards can help
beginning readers with fluency and speed. Phonics
are very important, but a little wait-time practice with flash cards
can make common, short words a quick, automatic "read." The easier reading
becomes, the more likely your child will learn to enjoy it.

Flash Card List!
For a widely used list of 300 words:

http://www.usu.edu/teachall/text/reading/Frylist.pdf

4-6 Favorite Books

Some young children have a favorite book. You know which one I mean. You've read it aloud more times than you can count. Wait time—especially in stressful places like the doctor's or dentist's offices—can be perfect for an already beloved and familiar book. When your child's favorite changes, though, be sure to update the book bag.

6-up Favorite Books

Rereading beloved books is one of the secret joys of literacy. In school and elsewhere, there is little encouragement to reread favorites, especially if the reading level has been outgrown. Wait time offers a perfect opportunity to open a familiar book at random, to read part of a well-loved story.

If no one feels like reading, try making up your own stories. The first speaker begins the tale, then stops. The next storyteller adds a segment, then passes it to the next person. The improvised plots often result in laughter. The skill-building merits of group stories are profound. Stories require logic and continuity, and sharing them builds the same kind of bond that sharing books can build.

Too tired to think of story starters? Use these....

All ages

In a place much like this one, a boy lived in a big house. He loved it, except for one thing. It was too quiet. It was quiet when he woke every morning. He could hear himself breathing most of the time! He made a decision. The quiet was going to end.

All ages

Jennifer heard the odd sound just as she was falling asleep. She sat straight up in bed and listened. It wasn't a terrible sound, or even a scary one. But she had no idea what it was. She got up and opened her bedroom door. It was coming from the kitchen...

8-up

Jake was starting to hate birthday parties. His mother was a birthday party clown, and she had talked him into being her helper. Usually he didn't mind, and she even paid him sometimes. But today he had to go help at Marcy Collins' house. Marcy Collins! She hadn't spoken to him since first grade. And he didn't blame her.

All ages

The truth was, Katie couldn't run any faster. All she could do was stop, double over and breathe, then stand up and watch the car disappearing. She took a deep breath and started walking.

6

One Family, One Book

Following super-librarian Nancy Pearl's incredible concept, cities across America have sponsored One City, One Book projects. The whole-city conversation that begins when thousands of people read the same book at the same time is remarkable. Encouraging community and reading at the same time—what could be better? In the summertime—or during the holiday break—try a smaller version of this grand event.
Share a book with your family.

THE ONE-BOOK,
FOUR-STEPS BASICS

- - - - - - - - - -

1. Choose your family! Think big! Grandparents and extended family members might want to be part of your book event. Neighbors and friends might welcome the chance to share a book with other families.

2. Or think small and keep your book-sharing experience an intimate one that brings your family closer together.

3. Agree on a timetable. Anyone who participates agrees to read the book by a certain date. Make sure there is enough time—if it turns into a stressful event, it won't be fun.

4. Choose a great book—or two! If your children's ages span enough years, you might want to choose two great books—one picture book to be shared with all and a novel or nonfiction book for older readers.

BOOK SELECTION

- - - - - - - - - -

How do you decide
what to read?

1. Make a list.

Consider all the options. Sometimes
young children are excited to read
something you—or their grandparents—
read as a child. Older kids will probably
be more influenced by friends' suggestions.
You might want to read award-winning literature
or a book with a particular theme.

Ask teachers, librarians, and booksellers for suggestions.

BOOK LIST

GREAT
EXPECTATIONS

WHERE THE
WILD THINGS ARE

PRIDE &
PREJUDICE

A TALE OF
TWO CITIES

HUCK
FINN

MOBY
DICK

You can learn more about suggested titles by reading reviews. These review journals all address children's books. Most have online archives.

School Library Journal http://www.schoollibraryjournal.com/
Booklist will soon be online. Sign up to be notified. http://booklistonline.com/
Kirkus http://www.kirkusreviews.com/kirkusreviews/index.jsp
VOYA (for teen and young adults reviews) http://www.voya.com/
Hornbook (a literary journal)
   http://www.hbook.com/publications/magazine/default.asp
Children's Book Council http://www.cbcbooks.org/

BOOK RECOMMENDATIONS

Valerie & Walter's Best Books for Children:
A lively, opinionated guide by Walter M. Mayes and Valerie Lewis

1. To broaden your readers' horizons, try a wonderful book written by two people I admire and love (who happen to be two of America's most informed champions of children's books). This is a user-friendly guide to more than 2,000 books for children from birth to age thirteen.

THE ASSOCIATION FOR LIBRARY SERVICE TO CHILDREN (ALSC)

This is a list of wonderful lists! Books are organized by topic, age, genre, etc.

   http://www.ala.org/ala/alsc/alscresources/booklists/booklists.htm

2. Make a Short List.

Once you have a list of suggestions, the real decision-making process begins. For older readers, let each reader suggest one or two books. Read a few pages of each aloud. For younger or emerging readers, look at the first few pages of the picture or early chapter books together and read a little text.

3. Decision Day.

For a mixed-age group, explain that compromises will have to be made to include everyone. Sometimes two lists—and two selections—is the only fair solution. It won't be easy to decide. There are so many good books! In every stage of the process, encourage participation and group decisions. For a stalemate, hold a vote or discuss compromises.

GET THOSE BOOKS!

- - - - - - - - - -

Once you know what book or books you want to read, you will need to find a copy for each reader.

Used bookstores, libraries, and online sources make it more affordable. Cheaper books! Yeah!

No used bookstore nearby? These booksellers deal in used books for children and adults. Prices of used books vary by rarity, edition, and condition of the book.

Try

Alibris: http://www.alibris.com/

Half.com: http://www.half.ebay.com/

Abe: http://www.abebooks.com/

Or try my favorite, a compendium search engine that includes these:

Bookfinder: http://www.bookfinder.com/

ONE FAMILY, ONE BOOK

Event Timeline and Guidelines

- - - - - - - - - - -

1. Have fun!

The idea is to have fun reading together. Bear that in mind every step of the way. If reading together becomes a battle of wills, a chore, or a dreaded obligation, no one will enjoy it. Be flexible but keep things rolling.

2. Time matters.

Choose a time when you all have time. Christmas vacation, summertime, and spring break offer opportunities. Make sure to allow enough time for everyone in the family to finish. Once you set the dates, lead by example.
Set aside time to read: turn off the TV for an hour or two, go to bed early enough to read, etc.

One family's solution was a staggered start. The slower-paced readers—the mother and two of the children—reading four days earlier than the father and the two eldest kids.
The fast readers still finished first, but not by much.

3. Midpoint Check-in

Halfway through your allotted reading time, compare progress. Is everyone halfway through or more? Do you need to adjust the time limit?

4. Shhhh...No Spoilers!

Make sure the discussion doesn't start before all are ready. Take special care not to spoil the ending for readers who need a little more time to finish.

Book Day:
The Big Discussion!

- - - - - - - - - -

Find a place in your home to sit in a circle. Circles increase goodwill, eliminate hierarchies, and call on human tribal intuitions and campfire cooperation. Try it. You'll like it. If it is a warm summer night and you have a backyard, circle up on the grass around a lantern or a few candles. If you live where you can safely build a campfire, I recommend it.

Inside, rearrange furniture a little to make room, or at least sit facing each other around a table or on couches. Make everyone comfortable. Make everyone welcome.

A big bowl of popcorn never, ever hurts.

Basic Discussion Guidelines

1. Respect is given to each speaker.

2. No opinion is right, nor is any opinion wrong.

3. Every reader will have a chance to say whatever he wants to say about the book.

4. All comments are to be heard by everyone in the group—and responded to by anyone who cares to respond. Private discussions can happen later.

Getting Started

What did you like?

You can begin with a simple statement from each reader that completes this thought: "This is what I liked about the book...." Some of your readers will like the book better than others, of course. By starting with positive comments, you set a tone of friendly acceptance and polite exchange.

What didn't you like?

Go around the circle a second time to find out what each reader liked less—or truly didn't like—about the book. Listen intently while your children talk. Each speaker should be able to speak into attentive silence. Remind younger and more eager readers that their turn will come.

Beneath the surface.

You can use the following prompts to help guide the discussion into deeper waters—but don't use them to limit the discussion. If your readers all jump in with both feet and respect is shown for all opinions and contributions, sit back and let the discussion fly.

What did you admire about the main character?

What didn't you like about the main character?

Did the main character have traits or feelings like your own?

Was there a secondary character in the book you felt drawn to?

Did you dislike any of the characters?

What do you think the author was trying to say about life?

Did you think the book ended in the right place?

How did the ending make you feel?

What do you think happened to the characters after the ending?

Would you read another book by the same author?

Last lap.

Go around the circle a final time so that each reader can add or modify anything she likes. If a reader has nothing more to say, let her pass without urging. There is no assignment to be completed—just a group experience, which will be different for each person involved.

Finish the popcorn.

Try not to call a formal halt to the meeting. In fact, try to let it fade rather than end. Booktalk can spur familytalk, friendtalk, siblingtalk, schooltalk, world-issue-talk... Leave the TV off for as long as you can.

BOOK 'EM...EARLY AND OFTEN

- - - - - - - - - -

Consider scheduling the next group-read while you are still sitting in the circle, even if it is months away. Ask everyone to start the slow, fun process of finding the next book. Informal mini-events can be held with as few as two readers, of course. Book-talks keep kids interested in reading. Keep the popcorn handy!

FOR MORE HELP

- - - - - - - - - -

Check out CHAPTER 12: PERSONAL PAGES for a sample response form some readers might want to use before the discussion. Let each reader decide what works best. The goal is for every reader to be able to reflect on the book and talk about the effect it had on him.

7

Friends Keep Friends Reading

Peer pressure works!

Get your children's friends involved in reading

and you will increase your child's chances of growing up to be truly literate.

Even the youngest readers and pre-readers will benefit from knowing their friends read, too. Encourage your kids to talk to their friends about books. Gently initiate the topic now and then.

"Tory loves horse stories. Do you?"

"Brian really likes books about dinosaurs. What do you like?"

"Traci is reading a great adventure series. Have you ever shown Alex your books, Traci?"

FRIENDLY BOOK
DISCUSSION GROUPS

- - - - - - - - - -

Getting Started

- - - - - - - - - -

All ages

Many of the suggestions for a One Family, One Book work well for a book discussion group for your kids and their friends. Be sure to check out these possibilities.

5-8

For younger readers, you can offer to help contact parents and host the meetings if you are willing and able.

8-up

For older readers, contact the school and ask if the group would be able to meet at school during one recess a month as an official reading club. The school librarian (or the parent volunteer in charge of the library) might be willing to sponsor the club.

Books that have been assigned for class reading can be a good basis for a discussion group. The teacher might be willing to help set up a group for those who want to talk more about the book than regular class time will allow.

All ages

Athletes and sports fans! Sports books will sometimes interest infrequent readers in forming a reading club. Instead of discussing story line and character, they can talk about what they have learned from a book they have all read. Discussion can range from which players are the best, the worst, the most promising; points of game procedure; playing skills; etc.

Shared hobbies can be the basis for a book group, too. Coin collections, dinosaurs, music—whatever interests your child probably interests other children among her friends.

If your older reader is interested in a specific genre, other kids probably are, too. A science fiction/fantasy reading club, a manga group, a horse-crazy club, a gamer's reading club where guides and cheat-books can be discussed, or a group that focuses on a single author's work can help your children keep reading. Younger readers will need a supervised place to meet, books to share, guidelines for discussions, perhaps a group leader. Tween and teen readers might want to stake out a few chairs in a coffee shop. Facilitate, if you can.

"I Loved It" Lists

- - - - - - - - - -

Readers are often swayed by what other readers think. *The New York Times* review section is nothing more than a venue for professional readers' opinions.

All ages

Talk to the school librarian or your child's teacher about having the students make lists of books they would recommend to other students. (Some already do!) Peer picks can be posted in the library or on a school website. They can be arranged by age-appropriateness, topic, author, etc.

6-11

Have your kids ask three or four friends (or ten!) to write lists of their four (or five or ten) favorite books. They can share lists or trade lists—or you could type them up and print them out as a single list of "Friends Favorite Reads."

All ages

If you have a family website, consider adding a page that includes book recommendations from your children and their friends. Monitor submissions and don't post personal information about any of the contributors.

GIVING THE GIFT OF LITERACY

Buying and receiving books as gifts teaches your children that books are valued, loved, appreciated. Gift certificates from a local bookstore allow a child to choose the perfect book gift. Involve your children in selecting the books you give to others.

Consider giving books for...

Your children's birthdays

Parents' birthdays (you could write a book wish list)

Grandparents' birthdays

Friends' birthdays

Graduations

Baby showers

Year-end teacher gifts

Get well presents

Gift exchanges

Mother's Day

Father's Day

And every other gift-giving occasion!

3-6

Talk to your extended family and ask them to give books to your children. When a book is given, there is often friendly follow-up to make sure it was read, to ask if the child liked it, etc. Making books part of family life is important.

All ages

If you attend local author signings, consider signed books as gifts. Children who like to read often treasure them. I once signed a set of books for a librarian's granddaughter—five days before the child was born! Seven years later, I got a note from her!

8

Book Nooks

Giving your child a place to read can encourage lifetime reading...

and that is the greatest gift of all.

DESIGNATED READING ZONE

Designating a place (or places) in your home for reading makes a powerful statement. Without having to lecture or announce, you are showing your kids that reading is important. Like eating and sleeping, it is a priority in their lives and yours.

Once you have book nooks in place, treat readers the way you would treat someone deep in conversation. Approach them with care. Don't disturb them unless you have to. Apologize for disturbing their reading the way you would apologize for interrupting a conversation.

Getting Started: Where?

- - - - - - - - - - -

Most of us read in our bedrooms—and many of us don't read until bedtime. It's logical.
There is a door that can be closed to keep out noise and intruders—and at bedtime
the chores are finished and the house is quiet. Making a book nook in each child's
room is the obvious idea—and it might suit your family best. But not everyone has the
same needs—or the same amount of floor space. I've included three book nook
concepts. Adopt, blend, modify, or use them as springboards for your own perfectly
personalized book nooks.

SPECIAL PLACE BOOK NOOKS

- - - - - - - - - -

My childhood reading place was in an odd little room off the far end of our living room where a side porch had been enclosed. I loved reading in that room because it was a destination—no one passed by it on their way to another part of the house. It was hot in the summer and cold in the winter. I couldn't have cared less. Privacy was my issue.

One of my friends had a reading place tucked beneath a flight of stairs. Her father moved in shelves and a camping cot with a big pillow. The steeply slanted "ceiling" was so low we couldn't stand up. We loved reading and giggling in that tiny book-filled space.

Basements, attics, guest rooms, corners of larger rooms, pantries, garden sheds, storage areas—there are many possibilities. Carefully consider safety, and healthful ventilation, and make sure the place has an exit in case of fire. Beyond that, nothing is off limits.

FAMILY LIBRARY:
A MEGA BOOK NOOK

- - - - - - - - - - -

Some families prefer a single book storage area. Readers can select a book, then go to other parts of the house to read. Other families have a den or family room to fill with bookshelves and comfortable chairs. If you set up a single, whole-family book nook, arrange the shelves so that all children can easily see and reach books appropriate to their age. Pre-readers should be included with their favorite read-aloud books where they can find them—and they can begin learning to reshelve them. The less parental oversight is needed, the better. The intent is to create self-propelled readers.

Getting Started:
Book Nook Basics

- - - - - - - - - - -

No matter where you make your child's book nook, there are two major elements that must be addressed: book storage and customer service. If you make the book nook user friendly, it will be used—and you will save time in the long run.

BOOK STORAGE

1. Each child needs to reach appropriate books without a chair or ladder.

2. If your child is young and has mostly picture books, the shelves have to be big enough to accommodate them.

3. There should be enough shelf space to house all your child's books—precious favorites and current or passing interests.

4. The shelves should fit into whatever room you are using without blocking a doorway or window. This is basic fire safety—take it very seriously.

5. Encourage your child to shelve the books in some kind of order. Basically, it is best to separate nonfiction from fiction, chapter books and novels from picture books, beloved keepsake books from current reading. Current reading should be easiest to access. Be sure to separate library books from all else to keep life simple.

About Those Shelves

Inexpensive shelves can be found at flea markets, cut-rate furniture stores, garage sales, in your mother's basement, etc. If anyone is handy, bookshelves are not hard to build.

Lowes, the home improvement store, has a simple bookshelf plan on its website:

http://www.lowes.com/lowes/lkn?action=howTo&p=Build/bookshlv.html

Google it: a search for *"bookshelf plans"* (include the quotes to narrow and focus your search) will bring you more than five hundred hits. Some have free plans. Others charge fees. If you don't see what you need and know you need guidance, pack up the kids and head for the library or bookstore for plans that will ensure you can do it yourself. Parent-built shelves exude love and support. In addition to adding a personal touch to your child's book nook, you will be setting a great reading-for-information example. But purchased or hand-me-down shelves hold books just as well. Keep it fun.

WELCOME TO YOUR BOOK NOOK:
Customer Service

- - - - - - - - - -

Making your child comfortable and relaxed in the new reading spot is very important. Think like the manager of a great bookstore. You want your child to come in, browse, find something that interests him, and then settle in to read.

FIRST AND FOREMOST, ABOUT THOSE BOOKS...

- - - - - - - - - -

Within reason, children should be allowed to choose much of their own reading material. They are individuals with individual taste. One child wants every dinosaur book ever written. Another collects *The Magic Treehouse*, but his younger brother didn't finish the first one. The joy of books is that there are so many different kinds, so many reasons to read!

BOOK NOOK CUSTOMER SERVICE

1. Comfortable furniture. **Some readers love a cushy chair. Some prefer to read lying down. My mother gave me a faded chaise lounge cushion and an old pillow with a bright new pillowcase.**

2. Adequate light for reading positioned near the comfy furniture.

3. As much quiet as possible.

4. As much customization as is feasible. **The book nook should have whatever it takes for your child to feel at home, relax, and get lost in reading.**

5. For tweens and teens, customize. **You might want a low table—a place to set snacks (paper towels make good napkins). Posters, mementos, and other precious things might have a place in the book nook. If homework reading will be done in the nook, include a place for pens, Post-it notes—whatever homework tools your older reader needs.**

6. For younger readers, pillows on the floor or bean-bag chairs might be perfect **If a smaller child will be using a comfortable chair, consider an ottoman or some other foot rest. Drinks and snacks in the hands of small readers can often ruin books. Make a policy you can live with.**

7. Ask your readers if there is anything they want to add to their reading retreat. **A magazine rack? Folders for collections of manga or other graphic novels? If the request is reasonable, do it. The more personalized the book nook is, the more likely your child is to use it.**

FACE 'EM OUT

Every publisher, every bookseller, every author knows the power of facing a book outward so that the cover shows, not just the spine. People are far more likely to pick it up and read a few paragraphs—and sales shoot upward. For younger kids, face out a few of their choices yourself. For tweens and teens, encourage facing out as reminders to get started reading a particular book.

WEEDING THE BOOK NOOK

Librarians weed their collections and your kids should, too. Once a year—or as often as you need to—have your children go through their books. They will develop a core collection of gifts, treasures, and old-friend books, but most of what is on the shelves can be up for reconsideration. Set a realistic and concrete goal. Ask your child to remove a certain number of books, clear a shelf, whatever seems reasonable.

Reasons to consider weeding a book:

Already read and don't want to read twice

Outgrown

Tried it, didn't like it

Been on the shelf more than a year without being opened

Barely made the cut last weeding. Still haven't read it!

FINDING NEW HOMES
FOR OLD BOOKS

Book donations can be made to:

Libraries

School libraries

Classroom libraries

Hospitals

Homeless shelters

Juvenile correction facilities

Disaster victims

Senior centers

Literacy programs

Christmas gift drives

Thrift shops

Dental and medical professionals with waiting rooms

Google it: "*book donations*" "*name of your town and state*" to find local projects (Include the quotes to narrow and focus your search.)

Check it out: *Read and Release*: http://www.bookcrossing.com/ provides a very interesting way to give your pre-read books to the world. Both children's books and adult books are listed.

9

Bedtime Books

There is no more precious time between parent and child
than the moments shared in reading at bedtime.

All ages. Really.

I met a mother, 89 years old, whose daughter is 67. Every year at Christmas they reread the books they read together sixty-odd years ago, with a circle of grandchildren (and great-grandchildren) around them. If you already read to your children at bedtime, keep it up. If not, you can't start too soon.  Being read to is a treasure, a gift of love, an act of nourishment. Here are some suggestions to make a grand experience even grander.

READ-ALOUD
BASICS
- - - - - - - - - -

1. Don't wait until your child is "old enough" to be read to. **You can share simple, colorful books with babies. They love it. So will you.**

2. A book a day keeps all kinds of bad things away. **Make time for reading aloud.**

3. Notice what lights your child's eyes. **Colorful Illustrations? Rhythmic text? Funny books? Books about animals? Choose books accordingly.**

4. As soon as your child is old enough to help choose the books, let him.

5. Try on books at the library! (Or the bookstore!) **You can read picture books aloud before you take them home.**

6. Snuggle up. **The physical closeness of reading with your children at bedtime is wonderful and creates an association of love and caring with reading.**

Which Books are Best for Bedtime?

- - - - - - - - - -

One child might want comfort books with reassuring themes. Another might love spooky stories some nights. Some children love nature stories or science facts to drift off to sleep. And whatever your child loves this month—it might be something different next month. Like any other kind of parent-child reading, there are no bedtime reading rules. Do what works best for you and your child.

READ-ALOUD ROCKS!

- - - - - - - - - -

Find a world-class reader at library story hours or at a bookstore event—or attend a storytellers conference—and pay attention. One of the best readers I have ever heard was a bookstore employee who was studying drama. Another was a quiet-voiced man who barely inflected the words, but who timed them perfectly.

Start watching and listening to other readers. Your style will emerge over time and it will be unique. Experiment. Change styles to fit new stories. Have fun!

BE A READ-ALOUD ROCK STAR

- - - - - - - - - -

Voices

Some readers make up different voices for each character. Try it. Start with "voicing" only the hero or heroine to see if you—and your child—like it. Be brave. If the characters are animals, roar like a lion and squeak like a mouse. Your child will almost certainly love it!

Volume Control

Raise your voice a little for a dramatic part of the story, or drop it to a whisper. Experiment and have fun with this simple, effective reading skill.

Rhythm

Change gears. Slow your reading speed to emphasize portions of the text, then speed up when the text is exciting, describing action, or mounting tension.

The Dramatic Pause

Children love to have a moment's tension before the next page is turned and the story carries on. Choose the most dramatic page-turns to emphasize with a moment's silence. Authors and illustrators work with this in mind—you will find plenty of places to pause for a few seconds to increase the excitement. Some readers will ask the listeners to guess what happens next, then will turn the page.

Eye Contact

Look up from the book at every chance and meet your child's eyes. Reading a picture book aloud is a conversation between the reader, the listener, the author, and the artist. There are almost always silent stories in the art. Look for them.

Audience Participation

When a young child knows and loves a book, she will often enjoy telling you (one more time) what is about to happen. When there is a repeated refrain in the text, some children love to join in.

Take Turns Reading

If your child wants to read, let her! Let her read a few words, or a few lines, depending on her skill level, then compliment her and take over for a bit so that the story doesn't lag. Read and repeat.

Encourage Sibling Read-Alouds at Bedtime...

...and cousins and grandparents and sleep-over friends and all manner of connecteds and beloveds. Share special books, pass them down from one child to the next. Reading together at bedtime is a special bond builder for the whole family.

How can you find great bedtime books?

How else? Ask librarians, teachers, and independent booksellers. They can all recommend specific topics, special story types to suit your child's taste. Check the review journals at your library to see what's new and good.

Attending story times at your library and local bookstore events will introduce your child to a variety of stories, old and new. When she is delighted, borrow or buy the book—or write down the title and the author for later.

Google it: Amazon.com uses a massive, friendly database. Type "any author's name" (using quotes to focus the results) into the BOOKS search bar. The results will show virtually everything the author has ever written, old and new. Type in "*bedtime books*" and you will get about 1,700 results!

You might discover a book—or remember one from your own childhood—that is no longer in print. These online booksellers have organized the inventories of thousands of small used and rare bookstores into a single database. Prices of used books vary by rarity, edition, and condition of the book.

Alibris: http://www.alibris.com/

Half.com: http://www.half.ebay.com/

Abe: http://www.abebooks.com/

Or try my favorite, a compendium search engine
that includes all of these:
Bookfinder: http://www.bookfinder.com/

THE BEDTIME YAWN:

This one again?

- - - - - - - - - -

Some children decide on a favorite and want you to read it over and over. And over and over. The ritual of reading the same book together night after night becomes important to some children. Even if you are bored by the repetition, your child is fascinated with the story—or perhaps comforted by it. If you like, read two books. Introduce something new, then read the favorite for the hundredth time before kissing your child goodnight. Deep breath, Mama and Papa Bear. This, too, shall pass.

10

It Ain't Literature-
and Kids Love It

What you think of as normal childhood reading depends a lot on

when you were born. Here's a very quick history of

American Poplit, Junklit, Sillylit, and Beloved Series.

DIME NOVELS
and
PENNY DREADFULS

- - - - - - - - - -

The 1800s

Dime novels were printed on cheap paper and written by authors whose literary worth—and research—was questionable. Tales of gunfighters and cowboys were written by people who never left New York City. Articles warned parents to protect their teenaged children's mental and physical health from the "false emotions" stirred by these exciting, affordable books. The books were wildly popular.

Legit at Last!

Stanford University has a dime novel and story paper collection of more than 8,000 items. You can check out antique fun-reading online at:

http://www-sul.stanford.edu/depts/dp/pennies/home.html

THE 1900S PULP FICTION

- - - - - - - - - -

Pulp fiction ousted dime novels in the late 1800s. Light, fun writing for younger children increased, too. Frank Baum's *The Wonderful Wizard of Oz* was first published in 1900—and the still-popular series added thirty-nine more titles!

By the 1920s, adults were reading romances and mysteries. Mass market fiction for children was booming, too. In 1929 Mildred Augustine Wirt Benson wrote the first *Nancy Drew* book and Leslie McFarlane wrote the first three *Hardy Boys* books. They both worked for Edward Stratemeyer, the man who created the series. Carolyn Keene and Frank W. Dixon were pen names.

The series concept worked wonders for some early readers and it still does. Kids love entertaining, fast-paced books—even if they were written decades ago in a world very different from our own. Try the pulp-classics on your kids!

Google it: "*Nancy Drew*" (use quotes to focus the search). Prepare to be amazed. The teen sleuth has been around more than 75 years and she still has millions of fans worldwide.

Google it: "*Hardy Boys*" and be amazed a second time. Nancy and the famous Hardy brothers have both undergone a recent extreme makeover (not their first) and now star in their own graphic novels.

Google it: "*The Wizard of Oz*" generates 2.3 million hits on the Internet. The movie, made in 1939, accounts for many of them. The first edition of the novel is a prized collector's item.

COMICS

Comic books were born in the 1940s to 1950s. They were banned from schools. A child caught with a Spider-Man comic book was sent to the office! Teachers seemed convinced that the popularity of comics meant the end of literacy. But Stan Lee and other comic book writers were vindicated over time. Comic books didn't damage students' ability to read. In fact, many kids remember comics being their gateway into reading. They loved the art, and they loved the stories. Superheroes seemed to encourage and inspire a generation of kids facing a bleak world that had been scarred by World War II. Spider-Man's rebirth as a movie star—along with the X-Men, Batman, Superman, and others—makes it clear that the appeal of these heroes is timeless.

MANGA

Over the last 15 years, manga—comic books from Japan that feature stylized art, magical transformations, and amazing quests—have conquered the world. Sales are huge and growing. Tweens and teens love them, and many kids read manga far more often than books.

GRAPHIC NOVELS

Graphic novels of all kinds have been a growing art form for decades. Now they are exploding onto library and bookstore shelves. Once primarily for teens, graphic novels are now aimed at readers of all ages. Old and new media are mixing and kids love it!

Google it: "*Stan Lee*" (Include the quotes to narrow and focus your search.) Stan's vision of the hero inside every person has circled the globe, beginning in the pages of Marvel Comics®.

Google it: *Manga* and get more than 16 million hits! Many manga novels are "age labled" to make sure adult themes don't end up in children's hands.

MODERN QUICK READS

SCARY BOOKS

There was a scare-fare fad that brought us
Goosebumps, Fear Street, Spinetinglers,
and many other spooky paperback series.
While the latest fad has faded, scary stories still delight some children—and they
always will.

Google it: "*scary stories for kids*" (Include the quotes to narrow and focus your
search) if you have a reader who loves to shiver in the dark. Check out titles online
and at your library. Get advice from teachers, librarians, and booksellers to make
sure the scare level is right for your child.

- - - - - - - - - -

Dav Pilkey's *Captain Underpants* has kept boys laughing for years. His bathroom and gross-out humor has been an entryway into reading for many, many boys.

Bruce Coville, a beloved author who also writes more serious books, is a master at making kids laugh—and read. His titles—*My Teacher Is an Alien* and *The Monster's Ring*—have started a lifetime of literacy for many kids.

Jon Scieszka (chess'-ka) is another wonderful writer who helps boys laugh their way into literacy with *The Stinky Cheese Man* and other titles.

> **Check his Guys Read site:**
>
> http://www.guysread.com/

Junie B. Jones is a laugh-aloud read. Her blunt and hilarious approach to life appeals to many young readers. Barbara Parks, an author who also writes deep and wonderful books for older readers, has let her famous humor run wild.

A Series of Unfortunate Events is an odd mix of scary, smart, and silly. Tucked into the page-turning text are many literary names and references. Kids love Lemony Snicket and his books!

SOAP OPERA SERIES

- - - - - - - - - -

Series that offer fun, adventure, and a kid-level soap opera approach have thousands of fans, too. *Babysitters Club*, *Sweet Valley*, and many other friendship-centered series have long appealed to girls.

ANIMAL SERIES *Pony Club* and *Saddle Club* grab the attention of horse-crazy girls. *Hank the Cow Dog* is loved by many children. Ask your librarian for more series that star pets.

HISTORY SERIES *The Time Warp Trio*, *Magic Tree House*, **my own** *American Diaries* and *Survival* series and many others introduce kids to different eras in history.

AND THEN THERE WAS HARRY

- - - - - - - - - -

Harry Potter brought fun reading to a new height. Kids and adults worldwide share the books, talk about the plots, the characters—and worry about Harry's fate. Who knew third-graders would tackle a 400-page book?

- - - - - - - - - - -

Teachers, librarians, and independent booksellers can help you decide. Avid readers often like series because they can gobble up books and the story goes on and on. Reluctant readers are drawn to series because the plots are usually fast and fun. Try not to criticize whatever your child likes to read. Kids' tastes change as they grow.

THE MILLENNIUM MEDIA MIX!

- - - - - - - - - - -

Movies have special effects that make anything look possible. Reality TV (and unreality TV) mix fiction and fact. Music videos tell stories in three minutes. Video games let every child play at heroics. Kids are reading fewer books.

But gamers write message-board essays about their favorite games. They give tips to other players and brag about their skill levels. Kids from all over the world respond with comments and jokes. Kids email each other and text message constantly. There is a rising generation of bloggers, writing public diaries that range from personal to political and beyond. Graphics are increasing, but the Internet, libraries, schools, laws and so many other facets of human life are text-based. Writing and reading are vital human skills.

11

Bookspeak

A quick introduction to bookspeak, the language of reading

READING LEVELS

- - - - - - - - - -

Leveling means measuring sentence length, word length and difficulty, and other factors. Reading levels are usually written as a decimal number. Ex.: 3.2 means the second month of third grade. 4.7 would be the seventh month in the fourth grade. Sometimes these numbers are printed on books.

READING LEVEL CATEGORIES

- - - - - - - - - -

Picture Books *Birth-5*

A book, usually 32 pages long, meant to be read aloud by an adult. The content is for small children, but the reading level can be high or low. Some have 10 to 12 words—or none! Others have 1,000 to 1,200 words. All have art on every page; nearly all are hardcovers and formatted horizontally. Some are square. Some are fiction, some nonfiction.

Picture Books *6-up*

Intended for older readers. Content is more complex and there is often more text. Some are fiction, some nonfiction. Fiction picture books with significant text are sometimes called storybooks.

Early Chapter Books *6-8*

Written at the second or third grade reading level—
50 to 70 pages long, hardcover and paperback.
Formatted vertically (not horizontally like most picture
books) and much smaller, sized to be easily held by a child.
Typeface and short paragraphs create a "loose" and eye-
friendly page. There are often one-per-chapter interior illustrations.
The stories are divided into chapters—a milestone for emerging readers!

Chapter Books *7-10*

Written for second through fifth graders. Often 80 to 100 pages long and formatted
vertically. Text density and typeface are appropriate for more skilled readers. Hardcover and paperback.

Middle Grade Novel *7-12*

Written for third through sixth graders, the typeface and format are increasingly
"adult." Content is suitable for age group, and illustrations are rare. Hardcover and
paperback.

Middle School/Tween *11-13*

This is a recently defined segment of the student population. Middle schools serve sixth through eighth graders. Formatted almost like adult books, though the text is rarely as dense or as small. Defined more by content than format—more mature situations and dialogue. Middle school libraries contain both middle grade novels and works for older readers.

Young Adult

Young adult (or YA or Teen) books are formatted like adults books. Some are wildly experimental in structure and story line—there is a lot of brilliant writing being done for young adults. Many use first person voice and address the passage from childhood to adulthood.

Poetry

Books of poems and whole novels written in verse are common and popular. Age level is determined by content and text level.

Nonfiction

Factual books can be in any format for any age. Text level determines the readership. Illustrations are often photos.

BOOKSPEAK TERMS

ISBN number

An International Standard Book Number, or ISBN (sometimes pronounced "is-bin"), is given to each book published for commercial sale. The International Standard Serial Number (ISSN) system is used for magazines and periodicals. The ISBN makes it easy for bookstores to order books. It's a ten-digit number printed in two places on each book—the back cover (or dust jacket if there is one) and the title page with the copyright notice and publisher's address.

Out of Print

When a book's sales drop too low for the publisher to make a profit, they usually stop printing it. There are many ways to find out-of-print books for sale online. http://www.bookfinder.com is my favorite. Used and rare bookstores can also run searches for titles you want to find. Price depends on rarity and condition.

Publishing Seasons

Publishers usually publish a fall list and a spring list.

Frontlist

These books are upcoming or newly published.

Backlist

These books are still in print, but not frontlist. Some books backlist and stay in print for years. Most don't!

Review Journals

These major review journals for children's books are used by educators, librarians, and booksellers to see what's new and what's good.

School Library Jounal
http://www.schoollibraryjournal.com/

Booklist will soon be online. Sign up to be notified.
http://booklistonline.com/

Kirkus
http://www.kirkusreviews.com/kirkusreviews/index.jsp

VOYA (for teen and young adults reviews)
http://www.voya.com/

Horn Book (a literary journal)
http://www.hbook.com/publications/magazine/default.asp

Children's Book Council
http://www.cbcbooks.org/

WHAT DOES THE GOLD STICKER MEAN? AWARDS!

Newbery Medal

Sponsored by the American Library Association. Given to the author of the most distinguished contribution to children's literature published during the preceding year. Only U.S. citizens or residents are eligible. The 2006 committee is made up of fifteen people.

Caldecott Medal

Sponsored by the Association for Library Service to the Children's Division of the American Library Association. It is given to the illustrator of the most distinguished picture book for children published in the United States during the preceding year. Only U.S. citizens or residents are eligible.

Michael Printz Award

This award is a recent addition and gives much-needed recognition to books for older readers. It is awarded for a book that exemplifies literary excellence in young adult literature. Sponsored by the Young Adult Services Division of the American Library Association.

Coretta Scott King Award

The award commemorates the life and work of the late Dr. Martin Luther King, Jr., and honors Mrs. Coretta Scott King for courage and determination in working for peace and world brotherhood. It is given to an African American author and an African American illustrator for outstanding inspirational and educational contributions.

Book Sense Book of the Year Award

Book Sense independent booksellers nominate books they most enjoyed handselling to their customers. Separate awards are given for excellence in children's fiction and for excellence in illustration in a children's book.

Boston Globe-Horn Book Awards

Given annually since 1967 by the *Boston Globe* and *Horn Book Magazine*. Through 1975 there were only two awards given. One was for outstanding text and the other for outstanding illustrations. Since 1976 there have been three awards given: outstanding fiction or poetry, outstanding nonfiction, and outstanding illustration.

Golden Kite Award

Presented by the Society of Children's Book Writers and Illustrators. There is a Golden Kite Award for excellence in fiction and nonfiction—and the Sid Fleischman Award, given for excellence in humorous writing. The books are judged by a small panel of professional writers.

National Book Awards for Young People's Literature

The National Book Foundation is active in promoting good literature and literacy for children and adults nationwide. It gives the National Book Awards to recognize outstanding contributions to young people's literature.

Orbis Pictus Award

Given by the National Council of Teachers of English for excellence in nonfiction work written for children. The award is named in commemoration of the book *Orbis Pictus (The World in Pictures)* by Johann Comenius, published in 1657. It is thought to be the first informational book written specifically for children.

There are many more awards.

Most are listed here: http://www.ucalgary.ca/~dKbrown/usawards.html

KIDS' MAGAZINES

They are way cooler than you might think!

- - - - - - - - - -

Kids love getting magazines in the mail. The ones listed here are tried and true classics. There are many more.

Google it: *"kids magazines"*

(Include the quotes to narrow and focus your search.)

Amazon Search: *"kids magazines"*

GREAT MAGAZINES FOR TOTS, CHILDREN, TWEENS, AND TEENS

CARUS Publishing http://www.cobblestonepub.com/

Babybug stories 2-6
Ladybug fiction/poetry 6-9
Click science 3-7
Appleseeds social studies 7-9
Ask arts and sciences 2-4
Spider fiction/poetry 7-9
Cricket fiction/poetry 9-14
Dig archaeology 9-14

Cicada fiction/poetry 15-up
Cobblestone history 9-14
Muse/Smithsonian 8-14
Faces worldwide culture 9-14
Calliope world history 9-14
Odyssey science trends 10-15
Footsteps African American 9-14

National Wildlife Federation
http://www.nwf.org/

Wild Animal Baby animals 1-4
Your Big Backyard nature 3-7
Ranger Rick nature 7-12

Girl's Life, Inc.
http://www.girlslife.com/
Girl's Life life info and advice 10-15

Children's Better Health Institute
http://www.cbhi.org/

Turtle fun, health, and nutrition 2-5
Humpty Dumpty's fun, health, and nutrition 4-6
Children's Playmate fun, health, and nutrition 6-8
U.S. Kids fun, health, and nutrition 6-11
Jack and Jill fun, health, and nutrition 7-10
Child Life fun, health, and nutrition 9-11
Children's Digest fun, health, and nutrition 10-12

NEW MOON PUBLISHING INC.

- - - - - - - - -

http://www.newmoon.org/

New Moon written and edited by girls 8-14 *for girls 8-14*

STONE SOUP

- - - - - - - - -

http://www.stonesoup.com/

Stone Soup children's creative work *8-13*

NATIONAL GEOGRAPHIC

- - - - - - - - -

http://www.nationalgeographic.com/ngkids/

National Geographic's KIDS—interesting articles about everything *6-12*

SPORTS ILLUSTRATED

- - - - - - - - -

http://www.sikids.com/index.html

Sports Illustrated for Kids—sports for kids 8-*up Librarian's Best*

WEEKLY READER

- - - - - - - - -

http://www.weeklyreader.com/pubstore/

Publications for every grade level. Clever, wide ranging, and informative!

12

Personal Pages

Use these pages to list favorite books, keep wish lists, and more!

WISH LIST BOOKS

Birthdays and holidays are always just around the corner.
Ask your children to give gift buyers a little help. List favorite titles here!

Reader's Name

Title and Author

FAMILY FAVORITES

- - - - - - - - - -

List your kids' favorites.
Check back in a year to see how their tastes have changed, or not!

Reader's Name

- - - - - - - - - -

Title and Author

- - - - - - - - - -

_____ _____

_____ _____

_____ _____

_____ _____

_____ _____

_____ _____

_____ _____

_____ _____

_____ _____

_____ _____

_____ _____

_____ _____

_____ _____

_____ _____

_____ _____

_____ _____

FAMILY FAVORITES

- - - - - - - - - -

List your kids' favorites.
Check back in a year to see how their tastes have changed, or not!

Reader's Name
- - - - - - - - - -

Title and Author
- - - - - - - - - -

TEACHERS' BEST

- - - - - - - - - -

Ask your children's teachers for two or three titles they love!

Teacher's Name
- - - - - - - - - -

Title and Author
- - - - - - - - - -

_____   _____

_____   _____

_____   _____

_____   _____

_____   _____

_____   _____

_____   _____

_____   _____

_____   _____

_____   _____

_____   _____

_____   _____

_____   _____

SUMMER READING

- - - - - - - - - -

Name	Title and Author

ONE FAMILY, ONE BOOK
BOOK CLUB NOTES

_____

_____

_____

_____

_____

_____

_____

_____

_____

_____

_____

_____

_____

_____

_____

_____

_____

_____

ABOUT THE AUTHOR

- - - - - - - - -

Kathleen Duey has a passion for writing and literacy. She is the acclaimed author of several popular series including *American Diaries* (Simon & Schuster), *The Unicorn's Secret* (Aladdin Books) and *Hoofbeats* (Penguin). Her stories have entertained and enlightened thousands of children and young adult readers. Children with a thirst for adventure are drawn to her stories of young people whose survival depends on their determination and self-reliance.

A favorite among parents, teachers and librarians, Kathleen has appeared for speaking engagements at schools, bookstores, literacy conferences and book trade shows worldwide.

For more information, please visit:

www.kathleenduey.com

LOOK FOR MORE
GREAT TITLES FROM
BIG GUY BOOKS

- - - - - - - - - -

REX:
Time Soldiers
Book #1

REX2:
Time Soldiers
Book #2

PATCH:
Time Soldiers
Book #3

ARTHUR:
Time Soldiers
Book #4

MUMMY:
Time Soldiers
Book #5

SAMURAI:
Time Soldiers
Book #6

Escapade Johnson
and Mayhem at
Mount Moosilauke

Eugene Stillwell
Wants to Know

Father and Son
Read-Aloud Stories

Big Stuff:
BIG RIGS

Big Stuff:
MONSTER TRUCKS

Big Stuff:
TRACTORS

Big Stuff:
GIANT EARTHMOVERS

Big Stuff:
RACERS

Big Stuff:
RESCUE VEHICLES

Big Stuff:
DINOSAURS

Big Stuff:
SEA CREATURES

ABOUT BIG GUY BOOKS

- - - - - - - - - -

Big Guy Books, Inc, is built on the belief that literacy is a birthright for every child.

But in a world of highly visual, fast-paced video entertainment, we are losing a

generation of young children to growing masses of "reluctant readers." It is our

mission to create books that are stimulating and engaging enough to recapture these

children and instill in them the joy of reading and the thrill of learning.

http://www.bigguybooks.com